Fleeting Thoughts

Suze van Tilborg

BookLeaf Publishing

India | USA | UK

Presentation by *BookLeaf Publishing*

Web: www.bookleafpub.com

E-mail: info@bookleafpub.com

ISBN: 978-93-5761-152-7

First edition 2022

Dedication

For Mum, Dad, Lukas and Emmie

In loving memory of Opa and Opa

Acknowledgement

First, I want to thank the team of Bookleaf Publishing. You challenged me to write this book and made it a reality.

Second, I want to thank everyone who gave me feedback, showed enthusiasm about this project, and motivated me to keep going and finish what I started.

Finally, I want to thank God for blessing me with all the amazing people in my life and the inspiration He gave me to write these poems.

Preface

The poems in this book were mostly written because of a challenge to write twenty-one poems in the same amount of days. Some were written in five minutes; some took days of changing one word and changing it back again.

In the end, the poems describe my life, really. They describe how I see the world and the people in it, the questions I have about life. The good and the bad, the beautiful and the ugly, the light and the dark; it's all of it. Writing about all of this made me realise how far I've come, how much I've learnt and grown. It made me appreciate the things I have.
Most of all it made me realise that the darkness won't stay forever. The sun will rise and life will be good again.

all flowers grow
through dirt

all flowers grow through dirt
is what they say
to explain the darkness
taking over my day

all flowers grow through dirt
is what they say
to make the darkness
seem okay

all flowers grow through dirt
is what they say
but what if the darkness
is here to stay?

You

temptation, distraction
leading me away
deceiving, convincing
leading me astray

I turn to You
everything else fades

no weapon will prosper
no attack will succeed
Your unfailing love
is everything I need

He

He
made the stars
made the seas
made me

He
knows me
loves me
holds me

He
renews me
completes me
saves me

the wave

the wave
knocks me over
pulls me under
makes me lose
my way

the wave
keeps me standing
drives me further
makes me know
my name

sunflowers

sunflowers
bright yellow
dark heart
follow the sun
together or apart
facing the light
like yellow so bright
but still
a dark heart

a dream

i see
a glimpse
of your face
a reassuring smile
twinkling eyes
before you turn
and walk away
now i know
you're okay
and eventually
i will be too

to my younger self

do grow up
just not so fast
enjoy your childhood
while it lasts

do grow up
just not so fast
take it all in
'cause it won't last

you do grow up
oh so fast
and how i wish
i could go back

Kinsale

look
out the window
the big blue sea
the green grass
the rolling hills

look
out the window
the wooden fence
the gravel path
the sleeping cows

soak it up
engrave it
in your mind
soon
you'll have to go
and leave it all
behind

a little light

there will always be
a little light
no matter how
big, small
faint or bright
no matter how hard
it is to see
there will always be
a little light
to look at
in the darkest
of the night

how do you feel

how do you feel
is commonly asked
the answer
is commonly masked

how do you feel
a rhetorical question
an honest answer
not even a suggestion

i often wonder
is an honest response
actually wanted
or is it more a formality
not even pondered

time

so much
needs to be said
so little time
to say it

so much
needs to be done
so little time
to do it

but still
with all the time
in the world
so hard
to figure out
the words
the actions

so is time
really
the problem here
or is it just
the perfect excuse

the sky is on fire

Opa's poem

the sky is on fire
as the sun slowly sets
the longer you watch
darker it gets

the sky is a field
pinpricks of light
the longer you watch
more will ignite

the sky is on fire
once again
but now
for a new beginning
and not for the end

dreams

growing up
doesn't happen
overnight
it happens
when a dream
becomes just that
no longer a goal
only a wish

so

maybe growing up
isn't what it seems
maybe it's realising
we're never too old
to chase
our dreams

then versus now

don't laugh too much
don't talk too loud
don't take up space
don't be too proud

don't speak your mind
don't let them know
whatever it is
don't you show

but now
i laugh so hard
i almost faint
and speak my mind
without restraint

that voice was too loud
and i was too small
now i'm okay
and i don't care
at all

someday

and maybe someday
before she realises
life will be worthy

plans

nothing planned
the day fills up
don't know how
it doesn't stop

so many plans
so much time
no idea
how to make it mine

try to change
to fill the day
and find the time
to make my way

the rut

i need answers
why, what
where, when
do i get out of this rut

maybe someday
maybe never
maybe i should try
not to be clever

i should trust
whatever it is
someday or never
the plan will be His

to be a bee

a bee
hops around
flower to flower
all he does
all in his power
he knows his goal
he does his best
oh, to be a bee
to be so blessed

imagine

imagine
having to be perfect
having to be flawless
no room for error
imagine
all the damage
all the hurt
it would cause
good thing
we can imagine
instead of live it

grief

grief
is strange
there one day
gone the next
hits you like a truck
or like a gentle breeze

grief
is a reminder
of what once was
but now is lost
of all the love
with no place to go

grief
fills the spot
where you once were
oh how i wish
i could go back
no more grief
only you

the girl in the mirror

i looked in the mirror
and didn't see me
no recognition
who could it be?

the same dark hair
the same blue eyes
familiar face
must be a disguise

the more i look
the more i see
the girl i didn't recognize
wasn't really me

she had the same hair
she had the same eyes
but now i know
it really was a disguise

the girl i see now
feels more like me
not a hundred percent
but one day, it'll be